Before I'm Too Old

I Want To Pass On a Few Things I've Learned
For a Happier, Healthier Life

By

Maggie Lou Smith

Copyright © 2016 Maggie Lou Smith

M. LiClar Publishing Co., LLC
Monroe City, MO

All rights reserved, including the rights to reproduce
This book or portions thereof in any form whatsoever.

ISBN: 0997024747
ISBN-13: 978-0997024746

CONTENTS

Dedication	i
Introduction	1
By God's Grace	3
Were You Born in 1925?	6
Have Faith in God	9
My Health	13
Household Hints	17
-In the Kitchen	18
-In the Laundry Room	21
-Around the House	23
-Health and Wellbeing	25
My Favorite Recipes	29
Miscellaneous	39

DEDICATION

I dedicated my first book to the most important thing in my life, my family. I can't imagine where I would be today with my parents, siblings, husband, children, grandchildren, great-grandchildren, great-great-grandchildren, nieces and nephews. And, I can't imagine dedicating this book to anyone else but them. I also hold a special place in my heart for all of our service men and women, past and present. So many of my family members have served, that I consider the entire military family to be part of my own.

INTRODUCTION

I was born November 2, 1925. As it is now late summer of 2016, I am 90 years young and I can see 91 right around the corner. Despite my age, I still have great memories of the past. Like all of my siblings, I was born at home and my mother was attended to by Mrs. Lillis, a great neighbor of ours. Mrs. Lillis gave me my first bath and dressed me in my first clothes.

Mrs. Lillis' name was Maggie, so my mother, brothers and sister thought I should be named after Mrs. Maggie Lillis. The Lillis family always treated me like family. They had ten children; Richard, Dan, Margaret, Ina, Anna, Henry (Jack), Mary, Julia, Agnes and Ellen in their family, along with me, the informally adopted one.

I'm often told that I could pass for age 70, but I feel 65 and still do my own house cleaning and run the electric weed eater every now and then. I'm not much of a TV person, but I do like to play a lot of solitaire. It seems to relax me after a full day's work.

I like fishing, quilting and meeting new friends. I love giving to and helping others; it really is the most important thing in my life. I may not always appear to others to be very religious, but I say prayers everyday; if not for me, then quite often for our service men and women. I have always been a firm believer that prayer is the best medicine when sick. There are many doctors today who believe in prayer before they go into surgery or while treating a serious illness.

Over the past few years, several of my friends and relatives have encouraged me to write my memoirs. I guess they had heard me tell my stories and believed that there were so many things I'd done that most other women would dare not do, that they thought it might make a good book. I guess being from a family of seven brothers made me something of a daredevil. To this day, I'm afraid of nothing, nor anybody!

I wrote and published my memoir, *Life Can Be Beautiful*, in 2016. The success of that book, along with my continued thoughts about how much more I wanted to write, lead me to write a sequel memoir. Life is so much different from the past that I often wonder what it will be like in 10 to 15 years.

As the world is now it is hard for the younger generations; and equally hard for parents to control their children. There are so many temptations and evil in the world; drugs, sex offenders (molesters, rapists). There are way too many out on the streets and could be living right next door. These days one never knows who the good guy is. So many people think that someone is a good guy because he's really nice. We don't really get to know our neighbors and you just can't tell if someone is good by their appearance and friendliness.

So many of the children of today have both parents working just to make a living for the family. So many ill feelings; so many separations; so many divorces. All this leaves many little children suffering for love and care from their parents. Even when parents are separated it isn't the same as one whole family together; to spend time together, eat dinner together and sleep in the same house. All of this makes me very sad and I feel horrible for the children who suffer because of the mistakes their parents have made.

Many who read this will stop and think that life can, or could have been better had they worked it out. Sit down, talk it over, and try to make a change for a better life for your family, and especially for the kids. Sometimes all you need is just something a little different in your life. Move to a different environment if need be. Adults can only change themselves and their bad habits to improve their lives. Most of all for their children's lives and to be able to live with family togetherness and happiness.

If parents would spend time talking to their children about right and wrong in life at an early age, it would help. Parents need to let their children know that if they do the right things in life; be respectful, caring and helpful to others, they will have more friends and a more fulfilling and happy life. Find a good job, do good work and receive good compliments on a job well done and Life Can Be Beautiful!

BY GOD'S GRACE, I MADE IT TO 90

My brothers and sister looked after me when I was young. They took me everywhere with them. They taught me how to play ball, swim in the creek, fish, pick wild flowers in the woods, find hickory nuts and walnuts, build a play house, make kites out of brown paper bags, sled ride; just about everything a child could do back in the 1930s and 40s. All of these same things are available for kids to do today and none of them cost any money.

If one is discouraged or worried about something, they should ask for God's help. I don't believe I would have lived to be 90 years old if it weren't for God's help, which I've asked for many, many times in my life and many of my prayers have been answered. Not a day goes by that I don't ask for God's help with something; sometimes four or five times a day I'll say a prayer not only for myself, but for others who are in need of God's help and guidance to a healthier and happier life.

I feel there is no need for fussing, fighting, or getting mad at anyone or anything. I don't believe it is the best for one's health. What does one gain by getting mad or upset? Think about it! You gain nothing.

Throughout the years, I've traveled to many states, but there nothing like good ole Missouri. We don't have hurricanes, forest fires or mudslides like many of the states on the coast.

In 1953, my husband, Russell, bought an airplane. We never flew far from home. Occasionally, we'd fly to Illinois for a fly-in breakfast now and then. Most of my traveling was by car, train or flying on a commercial airline. Although, I did travel by bus to Charlotte, NC a couple of times when my daughter and her husband lived there. I went once to help them pack up to move back to Iowa. After taking the bus to Charlotte, I helped Cathy drive back in the pickup truck, pulling a U-Haul.

We often went fishing in south Missouri on the Gasconade River and always brought home catfish. Night fishing on the Gasconade was the best. I've been fishing there since the 1960's.

In 1973, I had to take a year's rest due to having rheumatic fever, which was leaving me with rheumatic heart. However, in 1974, I was ready to go back fishing and Russell, my late husband, and I west to the Gasconade nearly every weekend. We would either set up a tent, or sometimes just sleep right on the sand bar.

In 2001, my son Larry couldn't find anyone to go to the Gasconade fishing with him for just one night. So, at 83 years old I told him that I'd go with him. I gathered my tarp, sleeping bag and one set of clean clothes, fishing rod and tackle and away we went.

We arrived at the river about 4:00pm and put the boat in. We stashed our gear and headed up the river about three miles. We found the spot we wanted, tied up the boat, sat on the shore and started fishing. About that time, I looked up and saw a big, black cloud.

"Larry, it's going to rain here in a minute", I said.

"No it isn't. That's the only cloud", he replied.

About that time, it started raining and hailing. I ran to the boat with my hands over my head and grabbed a life jacket to protect my head from hail. The storm only lasted a few minutes, but it was intense. All from that one cloud!

We fished until about 1:00am and put down our tarps and sleeping bags on top of those. We put our muddy shoes in a plastic bag in the foot of our sleeping bags and crawled in. We'd pull the tarp over the top of us to keep the dew off and sleep for a couple of hours at a time and then wake up and resume fishing. We left the river about 8:00am with 27 channel cats, all caught at the age of 83. It was a great day and night for me and I didn't even mind sleeping on a sand bar!

In August of 2016, now 90 years old, I talked Larry into taking me back fishing on the Gasconade one more time. The river has changed so much since the last time I'd been there, but it's still a beautiful river. It's fed by cool, clear springs and has a swift current. The channel of the river can be up to 15 feet deep and either side of the boat might only be three or four feet deep. You certainly can't dive off the boat since there are so many trees under the water.

In the 1960's and 70's, we'd be sleeping at night and could hear beavers gnawing on trees. Then we'd hear a big splash as the tree crashed into the river. Over the years on the river, we heard or saw skunks, foxes; even the occasional cow would come out of the timber to get a drink. Sometimes right by us.

On our trip this last August, we put the boat in about 4:00pm, like always, but this time we had to go up the river about nine miles because there were so many other boats on the river. Some of the boats had really big motors, like the one that had a 150 hp engine. They stirred up the water so much that the fishing really wasn't very good. We only brought home two fish on this last trip. Larry caught a 3 ½ and a 4 pounder. Because of all the other boats, we just decided to pack up and head home. We left the river around 10:00pm and made it home around 12:50am.

I'd really been hoping to get back to the river to fish again and thanks to Larry, I was able to go. So much had changed since the early days of our fishing trips. The ferry at Fredericksburg is no longer operational. The Corps of Engineers now requires the ferry operator to have a river pilot license, so the lady that used to operate it just shut it down.

Now to get to the park above Fredericksburg, you have to go through the town of Gasconade. The park has rest rooms, but no lights. You can no longer sleep on the sand bar, but you can sleep in the park. Boat regulations have changed as well. These days' boats have to have a light, a whistle, etc. Same as the regulations on Mark Twain Lake. There's always a Conservation agent or Water Patrol present on the Gasconade River now. I'm just thankful that since I'm over 65 years old I don't have to purchase a fishing or hunting license, but I do still have to buy a deer or turkey tag.

WERE YOU BORN IN 1925?
Maggie Lou Smith Sure Was!

"The richness of life lies in the memories we have forgotten"
— Cesare Pavese

World News – 1925

- U.S. troops landed in Panama to protect U.S. interests.

- U.S. women announced a plan for worldwide appeal to promote a world court.

National News – 1925

- The American Automobile Association declared that women drivers were as competent as men.
- Nellie Ross (Wyoming) became the first female governor in the U.S.
- The inauguration of Calvin Coolidge as President was the first to be broadcast on radio.
- An Indianapolis driver, convicted of manslaughter, was sentenced to one hour with the deceased.
- A team of sled dogs raced 650 miles with medicine to save the diphtheria ravaged citizens of isolated, snowed-in, Nome, Alaska.
- The Grand Ole Opry began its 'WSM Barn Dance' broadcast in Nashville, Tennessee.
- The most popular music in 1925 was 'Big Band' orchestras

Sports News – 1925

- World Series Champions were the Pittsburg Pirates
- U.S. Open Golf Champion – Willie McFarlane
- Pro Football Champions – Chicago Cardinals
- Indianapolis 500 Winner – Peter DePaolo / First driver to average over 100 mph - 101.13 average mph
- NCAA Football Champions – Alabama and Dartmouth
- Kentucky Derby Winner – E. Sande on Flying Ebony
- Remember when Lou Gehrig pinch hit for New York Yankees shortstop Wally Pipp to begin his streak of 2,130 consecutive games played?

Cost of Living - 1925

- Average new home - $7,809
- Average yearly income - $2,239
- New car - $290
- Average rent - $20 per month
- Tuition to Harvard University - $250 per year
- Ticket to the movies - $0.20
- Gallon of gas - $0.12
- U.S. Postage stamp - $0.02

Cost of Food – 1925

- 15 pound bag of granulated sugar - $1.00
- Gallon of whole milk - $0.33
- Pound of coffee - $0.25
- Pound of bacon - $0.25
- One dozen eggs - $0.13
- Pound of ground beef - $0.13
- Loaf of fresh baked bread - $0.09

Maggie Lou Smith wasn't the only famous person born in 1925. She shares her birth year with;

- Bozo the Clown – January 2
- John DeLorean – January 6
- Paul Newman – January 26
- Jack Lemmon – February 8
- Yogi Berra – May 12
- Tony Curtis – June 3
- Barbara Bush – June 8
- Merv Griffin – July 6
- B.B. King – September 16
- Margaret Thatcher – October 13
- Angela Lansbury – October 16
- Johnny Carson – October 23
- Robert Kennedy – November 20
- Dick Van Dyke – December 13

The population of the United States was 115,829,000

Federal government spent a total of $2.92 billion

Unemployment rate was 3.2%

HAVE FAITH IN GOD AND THE BIBLE

If you –
- Are facing a crisis – Job 28: 12-28; Proverbs 8; Isaiah 55
- Are impatient – Psalms 40-90; Hebrews 12
- Are jealous – Psalms 49; James 3
- Are discouraged – Psalms 23-42, 43
- Are bored – II Kings 5; Job 38; Psalms 103-104; Ephesians 3
- Feel your faith is weak – Psalms 126-146; Hebrews 11

When –
- Friends seem to go back on you – Matthew 5; Corinthians 13
- Business is poor – Psalms 37, 92; Eucleastes 5
- You have quarreled – Matthew 18; Ephesians 4
- You are seeking the best investment – Matthew 7
- You have been given a great deal of responsibility – Joshua 1: 1-9; Proverbs 2
- You are making a new home – Psalms 127; Proverbs 27
- You want to live successfully with your fellow man – Romans 12
- You bear a grudge – Luke 11; Corinthians 4; Ephesians 4
- You need forgiveness – Matthew 23; Luke 15
- You are sick or in pain – Psalms 6: 39-41, 67; Isaiah 26
- You think God is far away – Psalms 25-125; Luke 10
- You are lonely – Psalms 21, 91; Luke 8
- You have sinned – Psalms 51; Isaiah 53; John 3
- You are concerned with God in natural life – Deuteronomy 8; Psalms 85-118

Where to Look in The Bible

The Shepard's Psalm – Psalm 23
The Birth of Jesus – Matthew 1-2, Luke 2
The Lord's Prayer – Matthew 6: 5-15, Luke 11: 1-12, 13
The Ten Commandments – Exodus 20, Deuteronomy 5
The Last Judgment – Matthew 25
The Crucifixion, Death and Resurrection of Jesus – Matthew 26, 27, 28; Mark 14, 15, 16; Luke 22-23; John 13-21
The outpouring of the Holy Spirit – Acts 2

A Prayer For Our Country
Author Unknown

Our Heavenly Father, as we approach the changes in our election, may we renew our faith in freedom and our devotion to democracy. Let us pray that the world may live together in harmony. Give Your guidance to the leaders of this great country so that they may govern wisely and justice and freedom will live in our land. We ask a special blessing on those who fought and those who died for this freedom. We ask Thy blessings for those who are serving in the service today for this great country.
This we ask in Your name.   Amen

A Prayer For Our Service Men and Women and Our Government Leaders
Author Unknown

Our Heavenly Father, as we go through this day; let us pray that the world will join together in harmony so that our leaders may govern wisely and freedom will live in our country. We ask a special blessing on our service men and women both overseas and here in the United States and blessings for those who died for this freedom. Blessings for our government people to improve their governing and make our country a much better place to live. We ask this in Your name.   Amen

A Daily Prayer
Author Unknown

God, help me through this day. Open my mouth when it will do some good. Listen to my neighbor's plea and not always demand my right. Help us stand in another's place and feel the pain they must have. Make me always keep my word, but bite my tongue about what I've heard. Weaken the words I must say and to remember the words I must not speak. Thank you God for hearing me today.   Amen

A Daily Prayer
Author Unknown

Our Father, we ask for Thy guidance and for Thy understanding. Remind us of our obligations as a citizen of this great nation. Make us aware of the needs and welfare of others. Fill us with your spirit, so for our responsibilities and faith to meet all demands. We thank thee Father, and pray that we are ever faithful to our country and to thee.
Amen

A Recipe For Daily Living
Author Unknown

Take equal parts patience and unselfishness,
And mix well in a day's work.
Sift thoroughly to remove all gossip.
Use plenty of complaint shortening.
Blend in a morning offering until all is smooth.
Season with humor to suit toast.
If this fails to make a good day, fault is not with the recipe,
But with the cook.

A Recipe For a Day

Take a little dash of water cold and a little leaven of prayer,
And a little bit of morning gold, dissolved in the morning air.
Add to your meal some merriment and a thought for kith and kin,
And then as your prime ingredient, a plenty of work thrown in.
But spice it all with the essence of Love, a little whiff of play;
Let a wise old book and a glance above, complete a well-made day.
Housekeeper's Weekly

Maggie Lou Smith

A Little Prayer On Growing Old

Let me age gently, Lord,
As others do I know…
And let my thoughts be tolerant,
My voice be soft and low.

Let me age gracefully;
Not bowed with weight of years…
Nor sad because my youth is gone;
And let there be no tears.

Let there be friends, dear Lord,
The friends that I have made…
And let them wish to be with me,
As birds that seek the shade.

May youth be near me when
The setting sun grows cold…
Bright youth to want my presence still,
Not thinking I am old.

Let me age graciously,
And peace to me unfold…
O let me smile and call life good
When autumn comes, and I am old.
William Arnette Wofford

MY HEALTH AND TREATMENTS THROUGHOUT THE YEARS

In 1970, I was working at the McGraw Edison Plant in Clarence, MO where they made heating elements. I worked in 180 degree heat inside the plant. After working all day, I would come out to my car in the winter for the drive home and it would be frigid cold. Sometimes in the single digits when I got off after working the 3 – 11pm shift. Going from extreme heat to extreme cold air, I came down with arthritis.

My neighbor lady, Dorothy Newlon, was going to Hannibal and thought she should get me some vitamins for the arthritis. I didn't know what else to do, so I agreed. She bought them at a health food store.

Dorothy got me some vitamin C, niacin and a couple other vitamins. It was the first time in my life that I'd ever taken vitamins, and I've been taking them ever since. Later, I took some classes on vitamins with several other friends. We studied the Shaklee brand, which are made for specific diseases. In 1972, I started going to regular classes about the benefits of vitamins and even started selling Shaklee vitamins. As someone who has never wanted to take medication, and even refused medicine that was prescribed by doctors because of the side-effects, I've found that vitamins work great for me.

I take two alfalfa tablets a day to keep the arthritis under control. Alfalfa is a germ fighter and is good for colds, the flu and fighting the symptoms of many diseases.

I take one lecithin tablet each day to help blood circulation, especially leg cramps. As I have two valves in my heart leaking and one pressed in, the lecithin helps circulate the blood through the valves so I have no pains.

In 2012, I had a stroke in the middle of the night. I sweat all the way through the top of my gown. I had to hold on to the walls while walking down the hallway. My vision was blurred and my speech was slurred. My son called the ambulance. As the ambulance was pulling into the driveway, I thought of the lecithin to circulate the blood to the brain so I wouldn't lose my memory and I wouldn't lose the use of my arms or legs. I took a lecithin as the paramedics were coming to the door. The female paramedic took my temperature and checked my heart. She was ready to load me in the ambulance and take me to the hospital when my speech came back and my vision was unblurred. I stood up and was able to walk just fine.

About six months later, I had two heart attacks. I took a lecithin both nights that I had the heart attacks and I never went to see a doctor. A week later, I went to see Dr. Yager for a physical as I was scheduled to have a cataract removed from my right eye. Dr. Yager gave me the physical and an EKG showed that I'd had a heart attack, yet I never had to see a doctor with either of them, as I had taken a lecithin.

In my 90 years, all of the medication that I've taken could fit in a quart jar. I use many old, home remedies. For a sore throat, I gargle with vinegar. Just enough to gargle without getting strangled. It can be diluted with water if the vinegar is too strong.

I take lemon juice for my gallbladder. The lemon juice helps to dissolve any gallstones that may form.

For several years, I sold a lotion made by a pureblooded Native American Indian. His small factory was in Hamilton, IL, but is currently closed. The lotion was called 'Super J'. The old Indian gentleman said that I was his best salesman. I'd torn the meniscus in my knee and it hurt so badly at times that my knee would buckle and I'd go down. A son-in-law at the time had some the Super J lotion and asked me to try it, so I bought a couple of tubes.

I had an appointment with a surgeon in Columbia, MO prior to using the lotion. I kept the appointment and had an MRI. The doctor wanted to go ahead and schedule my surgery, but I told him, "I'll heal it myself." I showed him the tube of lotion that I was going to use to heal my knee, and to this day, I've never had surgery. To this day, I still use Super J lotion to increase moisture in my kneecap to get rid of the pain.

If you are going to buy vitamins, it may be best to buy the higher priced brands. These are usually all natural and many of the cheaper brands are 10 – 15% synthetic. These may help, but not nearly as much as the 100% natural herbs, which tend to be higher priced.

I've learned that if you are on blood thinner you should not also take vitamin K, as it may cause blood clots. Too much medication, I believe, isn't good for you. Especially too many different types of medication at the same time. I've also learned that if you are on birth control medication, you shouldn't take it at the same time you take other medication or vitamins. Even aspirin or Tylenol can counteract the effects of birth control.

With macular degeneration in both eyes, I've learned to eat a lot of vegetables. I make sure and eat something green every day. I've had seven shots in my right eye to keep it from getting worse and the green vegetables are the best thing I can do for my eyesight at this point. Green vegetables also provide antioxidants you need to go with your vitamin C. You can't take vitamin C alone. You have to take vitamins A & D with it to aid in the absorption of vitamin C in your system.

High blood pressure doesn't help macular degeneration and, in fact, it makes it worse. So, if you have it, don't get upset or discouraged about anything and you'll do much better. Watch your diet when it comes to building high blood pressure and especially avoid fatty foods.

I could never see getting mad at anyone or arguing with anyone. Fussing and fighting doesn't help at all. Just think about it! My recipe for living to be 90 years old is that I don't drink, don't smoke and don't chase men; although they chase me and I run like the devil! That's what keeps me in such great shape.

When you start getting 'old', you don't want to think that you're getting old. You have to think that you're young. You have to act young and dress young and you'll live longer. If someone things you're acting like a kid, just answer by saying, "I don't plan to get old or act any older. I'll live longer by thinking and acting like I'm young."

At 90 years old, looking like I'm 70 and doing the work of a 60 year old, I feel blessed. I can still do four or five hours or work, rest a couple hours and then work a few more. In writing this, I feel I need to add a few jokes; it's good for your health to laugh.

A Dutchman was explaining the red, white and blue flag of the Netherlands to an American. "Our flag is symbolic of our taxes. We get red when we talk about them, white when we get our tax bills and blue when we pay them." The American nodded, "It's the same in the USA, but we also see stars!"

We must always be proud of our good old USA and pray for our service men and women and our country. One day, years ago, I had spent most of a day riding a lawn mower. I came to the house to shower afterward and my back hurt so badly I couldn't raise my feet to take off my shoes. I could hardly straighten up. I lay on the floor, folded my hands on my chest and started praying for God's help. Within a few minutes, the pain was gone.

The things in life that bother me the most the little children from broken homes. Many parents without jobs and therefore no income. If I had a million or two dollars, I'd share. As the good book says, "love thy neighbor", I love doing just that.

HELPFUL HOUSEHOLD HINTS
In the kitchen, laundry room and just around the house

Life is so much different today than when I was born, when my children were born and even when my grandchildren were born. Families are on the go constantly and it seems that for every household chore, there's a product to make the chore simple. It also seems to me that so many of the things we buy today and made to be disposable.

This hasn't always been the case, especially when I was growing up during the Great Depression. Resources were scarce and we had to make do with very little. When something was purchased, it had to be important and it had to last a long time. Of course, the convenience of products available today wasn't even considered back then. Most wives stayed at home and their job was to take care of the house and prepare meals. It was a full time job for sure.

Today, husbands and wives both work outside the home and are always on the go with their children. Housework and meal preparation are often afterthoughts at the end of a long, busy day. That's just the way things are and there a product for everything to make every chore and every meal a simple process. Even though this is the way families live today, I think it's important to know how to get things done without the modern conveniences. I want to use this section to pass along the things I've learned in my 90 years of life.

You never know when you might find yourself preparing a meal from scratch some day, or making a small repair around the house, or even treating a minor injury of your own or your child. Myself and many others managed to survive just fine for many years without the conveniences of today, and I wonder if young people today would have been able to do what we did.

In the Kitchen

- Sometimes, tough meat can be tenderized by cooking in tea.
- For stained coffee and teacups, use a pinch of soda in hot water and soak.
- To freeze cake, freeze without the icing. Add the icing when the cake is thawed.
- To keep cheese moist and fresh longer, wrap it in cheesecloth dampened in white vinegar.
- Line the veggie drawers with paper towel to keep the vegetables fresh longer.
- Vegetables keep better in paper bags than plastic bags.
- Vegetables lose their nutritional value if overcooked.
- To give your refrigerator a clean smell and get rid of stains, wash the refrigerator with a little baking soda in the wash water.
- When using the microwave to reheat leftover meat, place a damp paper towel over the food. The moisture from the damp towel will refresh the food. Don't leave in the microwave but a few seconds.
- If cooking in a pan on the stovetop and the food begins to burn, don't stir with a spoon. Simply transfer the food to another pan, add a little water or oil, and finish cooking. You can also add a few apple slices to help remove any burnt flavor.
- Soak the pan with the burnt food in cold water with vinegar.
- When washing a pan with burnt food stuck to the bottom, wipe as much as you can with a paper towel and then add a tiny bit of water. Place the pan back on the hot burner until the water boils. Wearing a hot pad, tilt the pan to the side and wipe away any burnt residue. Tilt to the other side and do the same thing.
- For salty soup, add a raw potato or a slice of apple to correct the problem.
- A little vinegar added to milk will sour the milk when the recipe calls for sour milk.
- To tell if boiling eggs are ready to take out of the water, I usually take a tablespoon, pick up an egg and if it dries immediately, it is hard-boiled.
- Add white vinegar to the water when boiling eggs. The vinegar will help keep the whites in the shells should they pop open.
- Add a dash of cold water, a couple dashes of skim milk and just a pinch of cornstarch to your omelets to make them fluffy and light.
- Peel onions under cold water to keep from crying while you peel.

- A pinch of salt and a clean eggshell in your coffee will make it taste less strong.
- Keep a slice of bread in the bag of sugar to keep it from hardening. You can also add a slice of bread once a bag of sugar is already hard and it will soften back up.
- To skim the fat off of your soups or vegetables, I use a paper towel. You can also use a paper towel to blot the excess grease off of fried foods.
- When buying a chicken, the skin should be plump and yellow for the best flavor.
- Soak your potatoes in cold water for a few minutes before boiling and they'll cook faster.
- If the meringue on your cream pie weeps, you've used too much sugar.
- Stale crackers and chips can be placed in the microwave for a few seconds and will be refreshed.
- When making cakes, cookies, etc, always mix all of the dry ingredients together first and then add to the wet ingredients.
- When refrigerating leftovers, cover with a lid or plastic wrap. Don't use aluminum foil on Cole slaw, potato salad, cucumber salad or anything with acid in it.
- Do not leave cooked food in an aluminum pan, you could get food poisoning.
- When baking a boxed cake mix, add a little whipped cream. It will make for a moist cake.
- For tender pork chops or steaks; after frying in the skillet, place in a baking dish with a little water, cover with plastic wrap and place in the microwave for a few minutes until tender.
- If canned pickles are too sour, pour a little of the pickle juice into a pan and add some sugar and water. Heat on the stove until the sugar is dissolved, cool and add back to the remaining pickle juice.
- When boiling eggs, if one should float, it is a bad egg. Take it out immediately.
- I've been told to keep bacon from curling while frying, place the bacon in ice-cold water, and then wipe excess water with paper towel before frying.
- Add a few grains of rice in your saltshaker to keep the salt from drawing moisture and clogging your saltshaker.
- An apple or part of an apple placed in with cookies or loaf of bread with keep it from becoming stale.
- Never place ripe tomatoes in the window (sunlight). They'll be fresher if not in direct sun.

- To get rid of odors in the garbage can, toss in lemon, grapefruit or orange rinds.
- When taking a covered dish to a dinner, reunion or other gathering; if it is cold outside, cover the dish with plastic wrap, place the lid and put a rubber band from one handle to the other to keep the lid on. If the dish or pan is hot, use aluminum foil instead of plastic wrap.
- When preparing a pumpkin for pies, start by cutting the pumpkin in half and removing the seeds and fiber. Place cut side down in a baking pan and add a little water. Bake at 400 degrees for 20 minutes. It's then easy to scoop out and needs no masking.
- When making banana bread or cake, substitute banana baby food for mashed bananas. Two small jars of baby food are equal to 1 cup mashed bananas. This is always handy if you have to bake on short notice and baby food is easily stored.
- If carrots or celery go limp before you use them, soak them in cold water for an hour. Add a very small amount of lemon juice or vinegar. Drain the vegetables and place them in plastic bags in the refrigerator until crisp.
- To soften dried pastry, place in an airtight bag for 24 hours with a slice of fresh bread.
- Before thawing frozen vegetables, run hot water over them. Drain all liquid and cook in fresh water. Add to soups, stews or cook veggies in broth.
- For cream that won't whip, add a beaten egg white and chill, then try again.
- To tenderize tough meat or an old hen, marinate it in equal amounts of lemon juice and oil. Let stand two hours and then drain before cooking. Simmer slowly in a little water with a few drops of lemon juice. Cooking with moist heat will tenderize the meat.
- Warm a lemon and roll it firmly before juicing. You'll get more juice out of the lemon.
- Wrap fresh veggies in a paper towel before freezing and they'll last longer.
- Save left over veggies in the freezer. They can be used in soups or stews.
- Chill chicken or meat before coating with flour. The coating will stick better.
- Try adding one part applesauce to four parts ground beef for moist hamburger patties.

In the Laundry Room

- When you hang a raincoat or jacket to dry, stuff the pockets with wadded up paper towels and the pockets will dry faster.
- To wash rubber foam pillows, place them in a tub of lukewarm water and light suds. Brush any stubborn stain using extra soap. Rinse in lukewarm water. Squeeze out between Turkish towels. Hang pillows on the clothesline to dry. Wash the pillows on a sunny day with a breeze blowing. If hung in sun they may fade, so you must be careful.
- Wash leather gloves in hair shampoo that is prepared for dry hair. The shampoo will restore the natural oil in the gloves and give them longer life and wear. Also makes them look better.
- To remove spots, it is best to try and remove it immediately. Many spots set with age. Always remove the spot before washing or ironing a garment. Heat sets many stains by driving them deeper into the fabric. When removing a stain, don't rub too hard or too long, as doing so may cause a white or worn looking place.
- You're going to need a brush for scrubbing spots. A toothbrush works great for small stains. In addition to a brush, you will need something to actually dissolve and remove the stain. Depending on what caused it, you might use vinegar, chlorine bleach, ammonia, baking soda, club soda or petroleum jelly (Vaseline).
- White vinegar can be used to remove chewing gum from fabric. If the gum isn't stuck too badly, you can freeze the garment and peel the gum off when frozen.
- Club soda works well for cleaning leather or suede. On suede, use a toothbrush following the removal of the stain to brush up the nap.
- Cold water and a little laundry soap can usually remove a bloodstain, as long as it's fresh. Once it's dried, make a heavy paste of meat tenderizer and cold water. Apply it with a soft sponge and leave on for 20 or 30 minutes. When the paste is dry, rinse with cold water.
- Always use cold water when washing clothes with spots or stains, unless the clothes have grease on them. Spray the grease spot with Fantastic and wash in warm water.
- I've used Fantastik (non-bleach) on my clothing for years, even on expensive dresses and blouses.
- Don't over wash your clothes, it can take the sizing out of the material and cause it to wrinkle.
- Extremely hot water can also cause your clothing to fade and shrink. Excessive heat in the dryer will lead to shrinking as well.

- When hanging clothing outside to dry, turn colored clothing inside out to prevent it from fading in the sun.
- When drying blankets, throw a towel or two in the dryer with the blankets. It will cut down drying time.
- A little salt in the washing machine is a great additive to help set colors in dark clothes.
- Although I've never tried it, I've read that hairspray can take out ink stains if applied immediately.
- Lemon juice or a paste made from cream of tartar will remove rust stains.
- I've used gasoline, kerosene or paint thinner to remove tar from clothing.
- Zip all zippers prior to washing clothes. This avoids snags in the washing machine and keeps the zipper from being damaged.
- New, colored towels should always be washed separately a time or two in case they bleed.

Around the House

- To get rid of ants in the house, make a mixture of the following;
    - ½ cup sugar
    - 1/8 cup borax

    Add this to three cups of water. Soak cotton balls in the liquid and then place on kitchen counters on a piece of cardboard or aluminum foil.
- To get rid of cockroaches – I just use Ortho insect spray, indoors and out, especially around doors and windows.
- To get rid of wasps and yellow jackets – spray with Raid!
- A spot of petroleum jelly (Vaseline) will lubricate a pair of scissors.
- Feed roses (bush) with banana peeling.
- To keep cats out of your flowers and off your porch in the winter, put out orange rinds or coffee grounds.
- When filling a gas can in the hot, summer sun, do not hold the nozzle down in the can. Doing so can cause the fumes to build up in the can and gas may splash up into your face and eyes. (I had this happen to me. I found my way to the house and got some cream. I went outside, lay in the grass, and poured the cream over my eyes. My eyes were a little red afterward, but no longer burning.)
- To keep tools from rusting, place two or three pieces of chalk in the toolbox. The chalk will absorb the moisture.
- When storing clothing, curtains, blankets or other material in suitcases or boxes, throw in a couple of sheets of fabric softener.
- If the ends of florescent light bulbs are reversed now and then, it will extend the life of the bulb.
- Club soda poured on a screw or bolt will help loosen it.
- A little kerosene poured on a saw blade will make hand sawing easier.
- Vinegar will soften and loosen old glue that you want to remove.
- Homemade fish bait
    - 1 jar wheat germ
    - 1 box strawberry Jell-O
    - 1 egg, beaten
    - Mix together and add enough flour to stiffen
- If you try to hammer a nail or put a new screw into something, stick the screw or nail in a bar of soap first. It will drive in easier.
- Have a screw that won't loosen? Heat the tip of your screwdriver and try again. It should come out easily now.
- There are kits you can purchase to repair a chipped porcelain sink, and they work beautifully.

- When turning off faucets, turn firmly, but not tight. If turned too tight it will flatten the packing in the faucet and lead to a drip. I've replaced the packing (a washer) in several faucets in my lifetime.
- If you get a small crack in a window, paint it with a thin coat of clear shellac until you can replace it.
- To locate a wall stud for hanging pictures, tap the wall gently. The sound will be different and will tell you where the studding is. It's usually 16 to 18 inches apart.
- Use non-sticking cooking spray for squeaky hinges.
- For small holes in your screens, paint with model airplane glue. They'll be sealed and invisible.

Health and Wellbeing

We did things quite differently when I was growing up during the depression. Not only did many families not have the money to see a doctor, we just didn't have the time to quit work and go unless it was something very severe. Medicine wasn't what it is today and most things were just treated at home. Some of these tips might be considered 'folk-medicine' or 'home-remedies' that have no scientific proof. But, I have used nearly all of them nearly all my life and I can say that they work for me. If you ever have any doubt about an illness or injury, please see your doctor. Also, consult with your doctor before you take any medication or, if you are already on medication, see your doctor before you tackle any of my home remedies.

I believe that most doctors today are trained to think that drugs and surgery are the only way to help their patients. Years ago, I'm sure they were taught a little about nutrition. Therapy and exercise are very important to us after surgery and in everyday life.

I've had 64 hours of training on vitamins and medications. I've toured the vascular departments in two hospitals and had some first aid training in my early years. I've taken a number of CPR courses. If you are hired to transport (paid money to drive them), anyone over 55 years old, the Missouri law states that you must have six hours of CPR and 6 hours of first aid training. Each year that you are for hire, you must renew your CPR and first aid. This is in addition to having a valid chauffer's license.

Sometimes, what works for one person, won't work for another. Many vitamins will counteract the effects of your medication. Additionally, I found, when I was caring for my husband; one medication can often counteract another. It took me about 10 days to figure out what was going wrong with his medications.

- To relieve sore, red gums, add a drop of tea tree essential oil to your toothbrush on top of your toothpaste. Tea tree oil is a natural antiseptic that prevents gum disease before it starts.
- To heal ulcers, eat steamed cabbage. Cabbage contains glutamine, an amino acid, which is supposed to heal ulcers. Steam the cabbage and eat at least one big serving a day for two weeks. It worked for me.
- To prevent yeast infections, add yogurt to your diet. Yogurt helps as it contain acidophilus (bacteria) which reduces the yeast infection.
- One time while flying to New York, I was deathly sick with motion sickness. A friend of mine suggested that I chew on ginger sticks. I tried it and it helped relieve my motion sickness.
- Sooth the stomach with peppermint.

- For a minor sprain or sports related injury, always apply ice instead of heat to help reduce the swelling.
- Relieve diarrhea by eating only bananas and toast
- For a high fever, bathe with cold water (NOT ice water). When my son Larry was born, the doctor had him bathes in cool water and placed a fan on him to bring down his fever.
- I've been told that the herb valerian is a safe herb to help you sleep at night. I haven't tried it yet, but I plan on seeing if it works for me.
- Birth control pills should always be taken by themselves, without any other medication. Many medications, vitamins and even aspirin can counteract the effects of birth control.
- I'm told that for hot flashes, try aroma oil on a handkerchief and inhale it when you feel a hot flash coming on. This will also relieve menopause symptoms. Also, Vera gel, intended for internal use, can relieve the symptoms of hot flashes. Take one or two teaspoons full before meals or at bedtime.
- To help keep your heart healthy eat dark, green vegetables. They are a good source of magnesium, which will relax the heart muscle and establish function. The heart will perform better.
- For leg cramps, I take a lecithin vitamin. Another remedy is to mix two teaspoons of vinegar with two teaspoons of honey in a glass of warm water and drink. Vinegar is high in potassium and low potassium can be a cause of leg cramps.
- I've been able to relieve a toothache in the past by putting whole cloves between the sore tooth and my cheek, kind of like you would do with tobacco. It takes a little while for the juice of the clove to come out, but the pain will subside.
- Cover grass chigger bites with clear nail polish to stop the itching.
- Put wart remover on poison ivy to keep it from itching or spreading.
- For a small wound or skin laceration, sugar is a good disinfectant. Granulated sugar will help kill bacteria and speed the healing. Smear Vaseline around the edges of the wound to hold the sugar in place. Then put a little sugar directly on the wound. Cover the area with a bandage and be sure to change the bandage once or twice a day.
- A niece of mine had a bad cut on her leg that wouldn't heal for three weeks. She finally took a bar of Ivory soap, wetted it and then smeared the softened soap on her cut. It healed right up.
- Regulate your digestion with honey.
- Sometimes a shower or bath just won't get rid of stinky feet odors. Try soaking them in tea. The tannic acid in the tea eliminates the odor.

- If you find yourself with food poisoning, eat bread. It will soak up the poison for quicker relief. A few slices should do it. Do not put any butter, jam or jelly on the bread, just eat it dry. If the food poisoning is severe, see your doctor.
- Drink 7-Up for a sick stomach.
- For a good portion of my life, I have gone out in the timber and cut saffron trees to make tea. Saffron will cleanse and thin the blood. It acts as a nerve and heart tonic and relieves memory problems. I wouldn't recommend it if you are already on blood thinner or heart medication
- To regulate your blood pressure, you should probably see your doctor. The doctor may prescribe something to increase your potassium and magnesium, but you can also eat plenty of fresh fruits and vegetables, especially bananas.
- To relieve a sore throat, gargle vinegar. It can be diluted if necessary. Gargle, wait a few minutes and gargle again. I've taken vinegar for sore throats since I was a kid.
- To prevent new gray hair, rinse your hair with vinegar water after shampooing.
- My oldest daughter had glandular problems for about two years. She had what was known as an inward goiter, which is a swollen gland on the inside of the neck. The swelling would cause her eyes to roll, foaming at the mouth and make her pass out and shake all over. Two doctors prescribed a nerve medicine because they thought she had epilepsy. After two years of no relief, I took her to a doctor in Hannibal who ran a blood test. The results of the blood test indicated that the issue was glandular. He had to order medication from out East and have it flown into the Quincy airport. We had to meet the plane at the airport and she had to take the medication within one hour of arrival. The medication was radioactive iodine and it solved the problem.
- For minor burns, apply a washcloth soaked with whole milk. Apply to the burn for 15 to 20 minutes. You can repeat every two to six hours as needed for pain. Make sure to rinse your skin off with cool water afterward or the milk will smell bad.
- While pregnant, avoid eating radishes, navy beans or anything that causes gas. This will keep stomach cramps to a minimum.
- For a migraine headache, take (100% herbal) alfalfa tablets. Take one the first morning. Too many at one time can be a shock to the system. Take two the next day; one in the morning and one in the afternoon or evening.

- Lower abdominal pain, or gas, can be relieved by grating fresh ginger pulp and mixing with a teaspoon of limejuice. Take a spoonful right after eating. I've also used lemon juice instead of lime.
- Always ask your doctor before taking vitamins. Vitamins can prevent many illnesses, but can also counteract medications your doctor prescribes. Always try to buy All Natural Vitamins.
    - Vitamin C – Found naturally in citrus fruit and green peppers.
    - Vitamin D – Found naturally in fish oils.
    - Vitamin E – Found naturally in wheat germ and vegetable oil.
    - Vitamin K – Found naturally in alfalfa.
    - Vitamin A – Found naturally in fish oil.
    - Vitamin B – Found naturally in brewer's yeast

SOME OF MY FAVORITE RECIPES

No doubt, you've used many of these recipes. They are all from different cookbooks, newspapers, etc. Hopefully, what I have written you'll enjoy cooking. After 75 years of cooking, I hardly measure anything anymore. I just know how much to toss in. I've used these recipes over and over in my life.

My Little Kitchen
By Louise Fritz

I love my little kitchen;
Here God with me abides
While making meals or scrubbing floors;
He's always by my side.

He lights the morning sunrise
That makes each corner bright,
And when the day is ended,
He draws the shades of night.

I love my little kitchen;
There's nothing can compare.
With all the happy moments
That I encounter there.

And though the rain is falling
Upon the world outside,
My kitchen's always sunny
For God with me abides.

Five Cup Salad

1 cup coconut
1 cup sour cream
1 cup crushed pineapple
1 cup peaches
1 cup miniature marshmallows

Mix all together and chill in refrigerator

Lime Salad

1 3oz package of lime gelatin
1 small carton of cottage cheese
1 small can crushed pineapple
¾ cup whipped cream or cool whip

Prepare gelatin according to package directions. Add pineapple. Let set until thick, but not firmly set. Add cottage cheese and whip cream. Pour into serving bowl and let set until firm.

Best Holiday Punch

2 quarts water
1 can pineapple juice
6 packages of strawberry Kool-Aid
1 cup sugar
1 can red Hawaiian punch

Boil the water and add the sugar until it is dissolved. Let cool. Mix all together and add 2 quarts of ginger ale at serving time

Punch

1 quart cranberry juice
1 can orange juice
Add water to taste
1 cup pineapple juice
½ cup lemon juice

Mix all together and add 2 quarts of ginger ale at serving time

BBQ Sauce

½ pound real butter (1 stick)
1 pound box of brown sugar
2 small bottles Brookes ketchup
1 medium bottle of Worcestershire sauce
¼ cup sugar
½ teaspoon liquid garlic

Mix ingredients, cover with garlic salt. Bring to a boil. Very good for outdoor barbeque.

Baked Chicken

1 whole chicken, cut up1 can celery soup
½ cup milk

Roll the chicken in flour to lightly coat. Sprinkle with salt. Place chicken, skin side up, in a baking dish. Mix soup and milk and pour over chicken. Add a few pats of butter and sprinkle with pepper. Bake one hour.

Champagne Salad

1 (8 oz) package of cream cheese¾ cup sugar
1 large can crushed pineapple, drained1 cup of chopped nuts (optional)
1 (9 oz) package of whipped topping2 diced bananas
1 (10 oz) package of frozen strawberries, thawed

Mix and freeze. Take from freezer one hour before serving.

Frozen Cucumber Pickles

7 cups sliced cucumber1 cup diced green pepper
1 cup sliced onion4 tablespoons salt

Put salt over cucumbers, onion and peppers. Cover with water. Let stand 2 to 2 ½ hours. Drain, rinse twice and put in jars.

1 cup vinegar2 cups sugar
1 teaspoon celery seed (can use mixed spices

Boil and let cool. Pour over cucumbers, seal container and place in deep freeze.
*Always use coated lids when canning pickles, tomatoes or anything acidic.

Crustless Rhubarb Cobbler

4 cups diced rhubarb½ cup milk
1¾ cup sugar1 cup flour
3 Tablespoons butterpinch of salt
1 teaspoon baking powder1 Tbs cornstarch

Grease 9x13 baking dish with butter and place diced fruit in the bottom. To make the dough - Mix ¾ cup sugar & butter. Mix 1 cup flour, 1 tsp baking powder and salt. Add to sugar mixture along with ½ cup of milk and pour over fruit.
Mix 1 cup sugar, 1 Tbs cornstarch & 1 cup boiling water. Pour over dough.

Bake for one hour in 375 degree oven or until crust is brown on top.

Pudding Dessert
(Great for a party)

1 ½ cups flour
2/3 cup chopped nuts
1 cup powdered sugar
2 packages of instant pudding (Butterscotch is the best!)
3 ½ cups milk

1 ½ sticks margarine
8 oz cream cheese
1 (9 oz) container of cool whip

Beat cream cheese, powdered sugar and whipped topping until smooth. Spread on cool crust. Combine pudding and milk. Beat together and then pour over cream cheese layer, spreading thin. Refrigerate until ready to serve.

Frozen Cranberry Salad

1 cup whipping cream   ¼ cup sugar   Dash of salt
2 Tablespoons mayonnaise or salad dressing
1 pound can (2 cups) whole cranberry sauce
½ of a 6 oz can (1/3 cup) frozen orange juice concentrate, thawed

Whip cream, sugar and salt to a soft peak. Stir in mayonnaise, mixing well. Fold in cranberry sauce and orange juice concentrate. Turn into a one quart mold. Freeze until firm. For easier cutting, remove to the refrigerator 15 to 20 minutes before serving.

Easy Cranberry Salad

1 pound cranberries   1 cup water

Mix and cook until cranberries pop open

Add 1 ½ cups sugar and 1 package of raspberry gelatin (dry)

Cool and then add one small can of crushed pineapple and ½ cup nuts. Place in refrigerator until ready to serve.

Cooking Green Beans

We use a cured ham hock. Cook until tender. Take hock our of broth. Add the green beans to the broth with a little minced onion. Cut rind off of the hock. Cut the meat off the hock and add to the beans. Cook on medium heat until beans are tender. If using canned beans, cook 20 – 30 minutes on low heat. Sometimes we add a couple of peeled potatoes (cut in quarters) to the beans.

Cooking Vegetables

For cauliflower, broccoli and asparagus, steam with a little water and butter on medium or low heat.
- You can add milk or half and half to cream the veggie.
- You can also add cheese to broccoli. Just heat and stir.
- You can use milk or half and half and add one heaping tablespoon of flour. Beat until smooth and add a little at a time, stirring as you pour over asparagus.

Potato Pancakes

3 medium raw potatoes   1 ½ tablespoons of flour
2 eggs separated   ½ teaspoon baking powder
1 teaspoon salt

Grate potatoes. Add beaten egg yolks. Add flour, baking powder and salt. Mix well.
Fold in beaten egg whites. Make patties. Cook in hot skillet in hot oil until golden brown. Spread with butter. Serve with applesauce or sour cream.
- Bacon fat is best to fry potato cakes in

Potato Pancakes made with leftover Mashed Potatoes

Add the two eggs beaten and make potato patties. Dip in flour and fry in hot oil or bacon grease.

Scalloped Oysters

2 cans (8oz each) oysters   Saltine crackers

Strain off the juice off the oysters to get the grit out, then place in a baking dish or pan. Add ¾ pound of crumbled crackers, a pinch of salt, a little butter, cover with milk and stir. Add more milk if needed. Bake at 350 degrees for about an hour or until brown.

Cole Slaw

½ head of cabbage   ½ green pepper (diced)
1 small tomato   1 package of Ramen noodles

Shred cabbage fine. Add uncooked noodles. Beat or mix up pepper and tomato.

Cole Slaw Dressing

½ cup oil   2 teaspoons sugar   2 teaspoons vinegar
Seasoning packet from Ramen noodles   Dash of salt and pepper

Mix and toss on vegetables when ready to serve.

Oven Fried Fish

1 teaspoon salt   1 ½ cups evaporated milk
1 cup slightly crushed corn flakes   2 pounds boned fish fillets

Dissolve salt in milk and water mixture. Dip fish in liquid then roll in corn flakes.
Bake on a greased cookie sheet in extremely hot oven (500 degrees). Makes six servings. Serve with caper sauce.

Wilted Leaf Lettuce

2 large bunches lettuce   2 green onions chopped
4 slices of bacon   1 Tablespoon sugar
¼ cup vinegar   3 Tablespoons water
Salt and pepper to taste

Wash and shred lettuce in hot bowl. Add salt and pepper, sugar and onions (I use green onion tops instead of the onion). Fry bacon until crisp. Add vinegar and water. Bring to a boil and pour over lettuce. Toss until wilted. Serve while hot.

Summer Sausage

1 pound ground beef   1 pound ground venison
1 teaspoon liquid smoke   1 cup water
¼ teaspoon onion powder or onion salt
¼ teaspoon garlic powder or garlic salt
3 Tablespoons Morton tender quick curing salt

Mix together and form into a roll and wrap in aluminum foil, shiny side out. Place in the refrigerator for 24 hours.

Take from the refrigerator and punch holes in the foil. Bake directly on over rack over a shallow pan for 1 ½ hours at 350 degrees. Freeze or keep refrigerated.

Spinach Salad

1 quart frozen spinach (chopped)
1 cup old English cheese (cubed)
½ teaspoon salt
1 ½ cups Miracle Whip dressing
½ cup onion (chopped fine)
3 hard boiled eggs
1 ½ teaspoons vinegar

Mix all ingredients, garnish with additional egg and cheese. Can add peas or ham. Serve while fresh, within 24 hours.

Spinach Salad Dressing

1 Tablespoon Salad oil   1 Tablespoon flour
½ cup water
Blend together and bring to a boil, stirring constantly.

Blend in
1 egg yolk   ½ teaspoon salt   ½ teaspoon dry mustard
¼ teaspoon paprika   2 Tablespoons lemon juice
½ cup salad oil

Beat until smooth. Cool. Toss on spinach salad when ready to serve.

Baked Rabbit

2 rabbits   5 or 6 potatoes (unpeeled and halved)
Salt, pepper and flour   1 can cream of mushroom soup
1 large onion   5 or 6 carrots   1 cup apple cider

Salt, pepper and flour rabbits. Brown in vegetable oil on top of stove in large skillet. Place browned rabbit in roaster. Add sliced onion, carrots and potatoes.

Mix cream of mushroom soup with apple cider. Pour over rabbit and vegetables. Cover tightly with foil. Bake in 300 degree oven for 1 ½ hours.
- You may substitute Pepsi, beer or wine in place of apple cider.

Fried Rabbit or Squirrel

Wash and cut up in serving pieces. Roll in flour until coated. Sprinkle with salt and pepper to taste.

Heat enough oil or Crisco in a large skillet to cover rabbit or squirrel about ¾ of the way. Heat, then add rabbit or squirrel. Decrease the heat to fry, turning often, about 25 minutes or until pieces run dry when pierces in the thickest part, usually the thigh.

Rabbit or Squirrel Gravy

Remove rabbit or squirrel from pan and keep warm. Add two tablespoons flour to the pan drippings (need just enough dripping left in pan to take up the flour).
Stir in 1 ½ cups light cream or half and half and simmer (may need a little more than 1 ½ cups cream).
Stir while adding cream until it thickens.

* Chicken can be fried the same way as rabbit or squirrel.

Egg Noodles

1 egg (beaten slightly)	1 tablespoon milk (or half and half)
½ teaspoon salt	1 cup flour

Beat egg lightly. Add milk and salt. Add enough flour to make a very stiff dough.

Roll out thinly on a slightly floured board or between was papers (one on the bottom and one wax paper on the top).

Flour your rolling pen so it won't stick to pastry. Roll up like a jelly roll. Cut into thin strips. Yields about 2 cups.

Baked Turkey

Wash turkey inside and out. Sprinkle with salt and pepper. Preheat oven to 325 degrees. Place turkey in roaster, breast side down. Add water and giblets or cook giblets separate in a pan of water or can of broth.

Baked Turkey (cont)

Add enough water to make noodles or dressing (about 1 ½ quarts).

Cover with aluminum foil and bake about an hour or two. Check and turn the turkey over, breast up, to brown, with foil off.

If the thermometer registers 170 degrees in the breast or 185 degrees in the thigh, the turkey is ready to take out. Save the liquid (broth) for noodles or dressing.

Turkey Dressing

1 box of dressing   stale bread   2 eggs   1 onion

Mix together six slices of stale bread (or heals), two eggs and three slices of medium onion, cut in tiny pieces. Mix with box of dressing and bake at 325 degrees until pieces of onion are tender.

Substitute Measurements

1 Tablespoon corn starch = 2 Tablespoons flour
1 teaspoon baking powder = 2 Tablespoons flour
1 cup sour milk = 1 cup sweet milk into which 1 Tablespoon vinegar or lemon juice has been stirred, or use 1 cup of buttermilk and let it stand for five minutes.

Equivalents

3 teaspoons = 1 Tablespoon
4 Tablespoons = ¼ cup
8 Tablespoons = ½ cup
16 Tablespoons = 1 cup
16 ounces = ½ quart
8 ounces = 1 cup
2 cups = 1 pint
4 cups = 1 quart
4 quarts = 1 gallon
8 quarts = 1 peck
4 pecks = 1 bushel

Maggie Lou Smith

The Kitchen Prayer
By Klara Munkres

Lord of all pots and pans and things
Since I've not time to be
A saint by doing lovely things or
Watching late with Thee
Or dreaming in the dawn light or
Storming Heaven's gates
Make me a saint by getting meals and
Washing up the plates.

Although I must have Martha's hands,
I have a Mary mind
And when I black the boots and shoes,
Thy sandals Lord I find.
I think of how they trod the earth,
What time I scrub the floor
Accept this meditation Lord,
I haven't time for more.

Warm all the kitchen with Thy love,
And light it with Thy peace
Forgive me all my worrying and make
My grumbling cease.
Thou who didst love to give men food,
In room or by the sea
Accept this service that I do,
I do it unto Thee.

MISCELLANEOUS
This and That I Want To Share with You

Words
Author Unknown

The six most important words in the English language;
I admit, I made a mistake.

The five most important words;
You did a good job.

The four most important words;
What is your opinion?

The three most important words;
If you please!

The two most important words;
Thank you.

The one most important word;
We

The one least important word;
I

Laugh a Little
Author Unknown

An Irishman, out of work, went onboard a ship and asked the Captain if he had any work available.

"Well," grinned the Captain, handing the Irishman a length of rope, "if you can find four ends to that rope, I'll give you a job."

"Four ends, yer Honor! Well now," he said, showing one end of the rope, "there's one end."

"That's right."

He took hold of the other end and held it out, "There's two ends, right?"

"Exactly."

"And one end and two ends makes three ends, right Captain?"

The Captain laughed at his explanation, but just said, "I said four ends."

With a wide sweep of the Irishman's arm, he threw the rope into the harbor. "There's an end to the whole rope sir. And three ends and one end makes four ends!"

Think You've Got Troubles?
The Preacher's Commentary Series, Volumes 1-35, S. Briscoe

Dr. Charles Allen, former Senior Pastor of First Methodist Church in Houston, tells of receiving the following letter from one of his members during a stewardship drive:

Dear Dr. Allen: In reply to your request to send a check, I wish to inform you that the present condition of my bank account makes it almost impossible.

My shattered financial condition is due to the Federal laws, State laws, County laws, Corporation laws, mother-in-law, sister-in-law and out-laws.

Through these laws, I'm compelled to pay a business tax, amusement tax, head tax, school tax, gas tax, light tax, water tax, and sales tax. Even my brains are taxed.

I am required to get a business license, dog license, not to mention a marriage license. I am also required to every organization or society which the genius of man is capable of bringing to life; women's relief, unemployment relief, every hospital and charitable institution in the city, including the Red Cross, the black cross, the purple cross and the double cross.

For my own safety, I am required to carry life insurance, property insurance, liability insurance, burglary insurance, accident insurance, business insurance, earthquake insurance, tornado insurance, unemployment insurance, old age insurance and fire insurance.

I am inspected, expected, disrespected, rejected, dejected, examined, reexamined, informed, reformed, summoned, fined, commanded, and compelled, until I find an inexhaustible supply of money for every known need, desire, or hope of the human race. Simply because I refuse to donate something or the other, I am boycotted, talked about, lied about, held up, held down and robbed until I'm almost ruined.

I can tell you honestly that had not the unexpected happened, I could not enclose this check. The wolf that comes to so many doors nowadays just had pups in the kitchen. I sold them and HERE IS THE MONEY.

Maggie Lou Smith

Be
Author Unknown

Be understanding to your enemies
Be loyal to your friends
Be strong enough to face the world each day
Be weak enough to know you can't do everything alone
Be generous to those who need your help
Be frugal with what you need yourself
Be wise enough to know that you do not know everything
Be foolish enough to believe in miracles
Be willing to share your joys
Be willing to share the sorrows of others
Be a leader when you see a path others have missed
Be a follower when you are shrouded by the mists of uncertainty
Be the first to congratulate an opponent who succeeds
Be the last to criticize a colleague who fails
Be sure where your next step will fall, so that you will not stumble
Be sure of your final destination in case you are going the wrong way
Be loving to those who love you
Be loving to those who do not love you and maybe they will change
Above all, Be Yourself

Last Will of Mr. Farmer
Author Unknown

I leave:

To my wife - my overdraft at the bank, maybe she can explain it.

To my banker - my soul, he has a mortgage on it anyway.

To my neighbor – my clown suit, he'll need it if he continues to farm as he has in the past.

To the ACS – my grain bin, I was planning to let them take it next year anyway.

To the county agent – 50 head of cattle to see if he can hit the market, I never could.

To the junk man – all my machinery, he'd had his eye on it for years.

To my undertaker – a special request, I want six feed and fertilizer dealers for my pallbearers; they are used to carrying me.

To the weatherman – rain sleet and snow for the funeral please, no use in having good weather now.

To the grave digger – don't bother, the hole I'm in now should be big enough.

Maggie Lou Smith

That Place In Our Backyard
Author Unknown

We had a place in our backyard with a little quarter-moon vent.
Remember little back-house where everybody went?
There were two big holes in the seat-board and a little one down low;
The wasps built their nests up near the ridge over the seats in a row.
A box of newspapers was there well in reach of the hand,
It looks kind of crude to us moderns, but we used to think it grand.
There was a long pole-pry in the corner to use when the pile got high,
You could sit and read the papers and occasionally swat a fly.
But when it came to winter, there was quite a lot of grief,
That time of year in early morn, you made your visit brief.
The seats were covered with the frost and the wind blew up from under;
How we used to stand it then, makes one stop and wonder.
You'd sit down so gingerly and hurry all you could,
And dash back fast into the house....most everybody would.
Then back yourself up to the stove and shiver now and then,
And sort of think how nice 'twould be when summer came again.
Summer with its odors, flies, wasps and smothering heart;
When nature called you could take your time, it really was a treat.
Company for Sunday dinner, you felt anything but gaunt;
Walking around the garden paths trying to look nonchalant.
Someone in the (doniker) their feet against the door.....
If people don't like company, what are the other seats for?

Old Age is Hell
Author Unknown

The body gets stiff, you get cramps in your legs.
Corns on your feet as big as hen eggs.
Gas in your stomach, elimination is poor; take Ex-lax at night, but then you're not sure. You soak in the tub, or the body will smell, it's just like I said, old age is hell.
The teeth start decaying, eyesight is poor. Hair starts falling out, all over the floor. Sex life is short, it's a thing of the past, don't kid yourself friend, even that doesn't last.
Can't go to parties, don't dance anymore, just putting it mildly, you're a hell of a bore. Liquor is out, can't take a chance, bladder is weak, might pee in your pants.
Nothing to plan for, nothing to expect, just the mailman bringing your security check.
Now be sure your affairs are in order and you will is made right, or on the way to your grave, there'll be a hell of a fight.
So, if this New Year you feel fairly well, Thank God you're alive; although Old Age is HELL.

Old Age is Heaven
Author Unknown

The body feels good, the legs get a rest, you wear arch support shoes and feel your best. No worries about monthly cramps, or the pill, aspirin and prune juice cures her ills. You spoil the grandchildren, yes all seven, then send them home to Mom, Old age is Heaven!
No dentist to visit, your dentures fit right. You wear bifocals to take in the sights. No worries about being bald or falling hair, just don your toupee or wig, and off to the fair. Ride the OATS bus to dinner, playhouse, Tiffany's or Waldorf-Astoria, Old age is Heaven, just like I told ya.
No time clock to punch, no alarm to set, just watch for your Social security check. Sleep 8 or 10 hours, maybe more, watch your favorite movie on TV or Dinah Shore. Senior centers provides entertainment for all, card games, parties, sing-a-longs, have a ball.
Baseball games, Starlight or Worlds of fun, there are free passes or reduced rates for everyone, or you can cuddle up, and turn the lights down low, just like sweethearts of long ago. Alone at last, no one watching, no one to tell, I say Old age is heaven! Certainly not HELL.

A Soldier's Pride and Joy
Pvt. William P. Yager, 87th Station Complement Squad.
Jacksonville Army Airfield, Jacksonville, Florida
Brother of Maggie Lou Smith

As soldiers often sit alone, thinking of their folks back home.
Knowing how grand it would be, to have a good old ten days leave.

If they get it and go home, they start off on the roam. They know what they will see, and how grand it will be.

Now as those days go by so fast, they begin thinking of the past. And on the last day at home, they know they have no more days to roam.

As that last day goes by, they begin to think and then to sigh. Knowing how hard it is to say good-bye.

Now that last day is gone at last, when back to the post, they think of the past. It was a great time I have had, but the last day was really sad.

'Twas a great day when I was home, I went every day on the roam. And now my roaming days are gone, and I am back where there is no fun.

I think often of the fun I had at home, when I went on the roam. But when I left it was so sad, to leave my dearest Mother and Dad.

Now the time has come at last, when soldiers never think of the past. They think of the future instead, when into the Japs they can throw lead.

To others it may sound bad, those rascals we want so bad, to keep from worrying our Mother and Dad.

Now when this dirty war is won, home we will go on the run. And our fathers and mothers will be glad, because they have been left so sad.

This is the future we will all look forward to, but we still know what to do. And as these Army days roll by, we have no time to wait to sigh.

Now we soldiers are on the beam, to beat the enemy at their scheme. Buying bonds is a good way, to stop the Axis from their play.

We are all praying for the day to come, when Hitler's and Tojo's rambling days are done. But, on and on we think how bad, to have our fathers and mothers so sad.

When this war we will have won, we will think of what we have done. We, the people, all will say, God Bless the good old U.S. A.

ABOUT THE AUTHOR

Maggie Lou Smith has lead a full, often tragic, mostly beautiful life. At 90 years of age she decided to publish her memoir. The book was a success and before the first copies rolled off the press, she remembered things she should have written. She immediately started on her second book, which is a collection of recipes, home remedies, household tips and important prayers that she wants to pass down to future generations before she gets too old and forgets. Don't expect her to be too old to tell a story anytime soon. Maggie Lou is in great physical and mental health and might just start on her third book soon.

www.ingramcontent.com/pod-product-compliance
Lightning Source LLC
Chambersburg PA
CBHW070038070426
42449CB00012BA/3089